I'm Just a Little Guy

How to Escape the Horrors and Get Back to Dillydallying

written by Charlie James

illustrated by Paige Tompkins

QUIRK BOOKS
PHILADELPHIA

Library of Congress Cataloging-in-Publication Data
Names: James, Charlie (Comedian), author. | Tompkins, Paige, illustrator.
Title: I'm just a little guy : how to escape the horrors and get back to
    dillydallying / by Charlie James ; illustrated by Paige Tompkins.
Description: Philadelphia : Quirk Books, 2025. | Summary: "A collection of
    humorous advice about slowing down and enjoying life from Paul Bog, a small
    frog"—Provided by publisher.
Identifiers: LCCN 2024053980 (print) | LCCN 2024053981 (ebook) | ISBN
    9781683694946 (hardcover) | ISBN 9781683694953 (ebook)
Subjects: LCSH: Conduct of life—Humor.
Classification: LCC PN6231.C6142 J36 2025 (print) | LCC PN6231.C6142
    (ebook) | DDC 818.602—dc23/eng/20241202
LC record available at https://lccn.loc.gov/2024053980
LC ebook record available at https://lccn.loc.gov/2024053981

ISBN: 978-1-68369-494-6

Printed in China

Typeset in Euroika Kamp and Louise Walker

Designed by Elissa Flanigan
Production management by Mandy Sampson

Quirk Books
215 Church Street
Philadelphia, PA 19106
quirkbooks.com

Quirk Books' authorized representative in the EU for product
safety and compliance is Easy Access System Europe, Mustamäe
tee 50, 10621 Tallinn, Estonia, gpsr.requests@easproject.com

10 9 8 7 6 5 4 3 2 1

For Ben Acker—CJ

For Stephen Tompkins—PT

Pleasure to meet me. My name is Paul Bog. I am a small frog.

Before I do anything, I ask myself, "Is this something a little frog on a lily pad would do?" And if the answer is no? I'm busy that day.

This is the rule by which I live my one
life on this wet, green earth. If you too
want to live like a little guy on a lily
pad, read on to learn from my example.

A Little Guy
at Home

They say home is where the heart is. I say home is where you keep your stuff. Your heart, whenever possible, should remain firmly inside your body.

Collecting Trinkets

Once my pockets have reached maximum trinket capacity, I like to carry a bindle over my shoulder. Anything can be a trinket: heart-shaped rocks, buttons, engagement rings flung dramatically into the river, your neighbor's mail, teeth from on the ground.

Pets

A pet is a little guy who lives in your house but doesn't pay rent. A pet must always be smaller than whatever kind of animal you are. I keep a cricket named Kyle who is classically trained in both opera and using the litter box.

15

Once I attempted to tame a stray beagle,
breaking the cardinal pet-to-owner-ratio
guideline. Huge mistake. We still get
lunch sometimes.

Cooking

You will need:

- An open flame you have little to no control over
- Pond water
- Bugs you don't know personally
- A large pot someone lent to you that you never returned because they called you "uncouth" at a tea party

Instructions:

1. Get distracted by a warm breeze
    that reminds you of a past lover and
    let the pot of pond water boil over.
2. Give up and pay a squirrel to deliver
    supper to your abode.

Staying Home with a Cold

"A cold" is something you say you have
when you want to stay home and gaze
out the window. Put strawberry jam
in a handkerchief for dramatic effect.
Remember: It's not lying if you call it
theater.

Hosting Guests

Sometimes, a weary traveler will ask to stay in your home. Typically, this is a friend or family member in town for a bread-baking competition.

I always offer to sleep in my sink so my guest can take the bed, but when they humbly decline, I am relieved.

If I do not wish to entertain, that is what the thirty-seven deadbolts on my front door are for. Unfortunately, they do not stop voles from digging up into my living room.

A Little Guy
at Work

I'm no good at jobs. For starters, I don't even want to be there. I'd rather be throwing my head back and laughing knowingly in a big field.

Interviewing for a Job

If, however, I'm saving up for a particularly intricate sweater, I will begrudgingly get a real job that pays real coins in a burlap sack. I gravitate toward roles that require me to wear a smart little outfit, like mailfrog or train conductor.

It is customary to bring your potential
employer a gift to show dedication. I like
to bring a jar of bees. Once my coworkers
see how much honey these guys can
make, they'll forget all about the swarm,
subsequent stings, and Mike's brief
hospitalization.

Your résumé is a great opportunity to show off your extensive work history. Mine includes baking bread, digging deep holes, and that one summer I worked for the CIA on an intelligence operation I am not at liberty to speak about. Fine, since you begged—I monitored a small pond for spies. I mean flies. I mean spies.

Self-Employment

If possible, be your own boss. I pay myself forty dollars an hour to listen to trees falling in the forest.

Between you and me? They make a
sound every time.

39

Handling a Difficult Coworker

Write down everything you'd like to scream at their face onto a large scroll. Roll that scroll as tightly as possible and seal it in a glass bottle. Tie a piece of linen soaked in scotch to the bottle, light it on fire, and throw the bottle into the sea.

Tonight, as your head hits the pillow, you are permitted to picture your coworker getting into a nonlethal bicycle accident. You are even permitted to smile.

Correspondence

Emails, texts, calls—all of them are to be avoided. Instead, I opt for formal handwritten letters and scrolls.

After all, little guys were never meant to be reachable at all hours of the day. Sometimes I'm busy using a toadstool as an umbrella and I need both hands.

And of course, in emergencies, one can always place a steaming apple pie outside my open window if they really need to get my attention.

Avoiding Burnout

For every hour of work I do, I spend three hours staring at a still life painting.

Frans van Estuary
·1582–1647·

If that doesn't do the trick, consider holding a big seashell up to your ear so you can hear the ocean.

This will fool your nervous system into
thinking you are on vacation and not
emailing with Linda from Accounting.

51

Saving Money

Sometimes I have a few loose coins left over after treating myself to a new porcelain figurine of a bichon frise.

I cannot save money for the future. The future is too unknowable. I can, however, toss a little coin into a nearby wishing well and hope for the best.

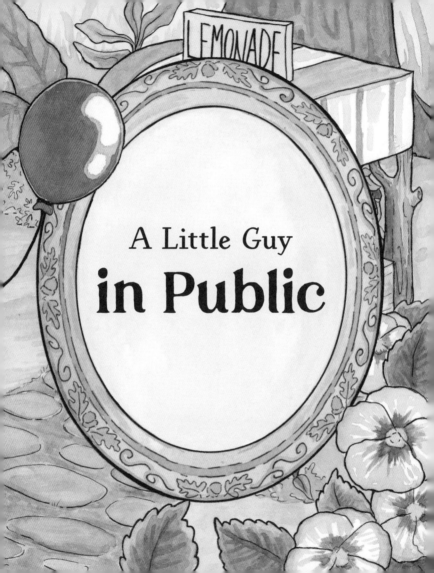

A Little Guy
in Public

Going Out

Ah, Public. The Private of other people. I'm told it's important to leave my house from time to time. But I am told this by creatures who do not live at my house and do not understand how cozy it is.

If invited out, I will begrudgingly attend with a mug of hot tea I brought from home. And yes, at some point, while gesticulating wildly, I will spill that tea on myself and on the floor. Apologies in advance.

While a tavern or pub of sorts is preferable, I'll go anywhere that has a live all-cricket band playing free-form jazz.

If a bar is "cash only," I recommend stopping by a fountain on the way over to gather coins.

Transporting Your Body from One Place to Another

Assuming a sailboat or fixed gear bicycle is unavailable, I will occasionally catch a train or hitch a ride on the back of a wayward fox.

If purchasing a car is absolutely
necessary, I look for a used model with
an old-timey horn. To avoid being pushed
around by a car salesman, I like to bring
along a creature that is larger than me.

DO NOT ATTEMPT TO COMMUTE
VIA SKATEBOARD. Little guys have
all the enthusiasm and none of the core
stability for that activity.

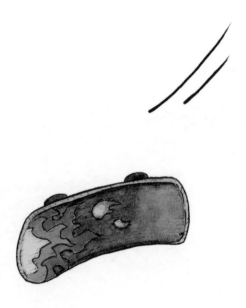

Bumping into Your Ex

I always wear my finest linens when I'm about town just in case I run into the snapping turtle I went on one date with ten years ago. He never replied to my last handwritten ode and I still think of him once a week.

Big Crowds

If you find yourself in a large crowd, you need to quickly take control of the situation. The best way to take charge is to get a chant going. Some of my favorites include: "Jam! Is! Jelly! With! Seeds!" and "Crows! Aren't! Emo! They're! Goth!"

A Little Guy

with Friends

Friends are creatures you'd share a baguette with. I cannot go more than a week without paying a visit to a friend or I will start to howl at the moon. This is terribly confusing for the wolves who live down the lane. For their sake and mine, I schedule a minimum of two picnics a week to keep lonesomeness at arm's length.

Accommodating Friends with Different Needs

While I desperately want to dictate the actions of those around me, I have been informed by a team of horse lawyers* that I should not. I cannot control other beings, nor can I change them into versions of themselves I find more appealing.

---

*Lawyers for horses, not horses who practice law. The lawyers themselves are goats.

I have a hunch that you can't either.
I'm sorry you had to hear it from me.
Birds will keep chirping. Bees will
keep buzzing. Possums will keep lying
motionless in a busy road during rush
hour.

Attending and Hosting Parties

Before going to a party, I always ask, "Will this interfere with me pondering my one precious life whilst sorting my button collection?" If the answer is yes, I will make up an excuse like "I can't that night. I'm making a tart for the sick and needy."

I like to brainstorm several topics of conversation in advance. I cannot discuss religion, money, or which haircuts are bad. I can, however, talk at length about beans on toast.

When hosting, a charcuterie board is the perfect snack for groups. Birds will pick at the almonds, mice at the cheese, and raccoons at everything that remains.

Keeping Secrets

I am a terrible secret keeper. What can I say? I love to discuss! I do my best to keep my friends' secrets private, but if push comes to shove, I will whisper the secret into a jar. If the secret is especially good, I will boil the jar just to be safe. This also helps with botulism.

Practice this technique at home using one of my secrets:

- As a tadpole, I stole an extra helping of moss, then lied and blamed it on one of my four thousand siblings.
- I've never heard a song and thought "this could use more bongo drums."
- I do not think highly of palm trees.

Making Enemies

All this talk of friends, but what of enemies? An enemy is a person who has inconvenienced you even slightly. Little guys must have between one and three enemies at any given time. One's enemies motivate one to work harder at their passions, be they line dancing or whittling sticks.

My current enemy is a raccoon who said my smoking jacket makes me look like an adjunct professor. I am working on finding a backup enemy. Unfortunately, everyone in town is very kind.

A Little Guy
in Love

Having a crush is when you want to go to the farmers market with someone. I avoid this feeling at all costs. It's a distraction from the important things in life, like looking at paintings of ships. On occasion, I will wave to the field mouse that lives on a houseboat, but I can't make eye contact with her for too long without getting a crush. Once a crush has formed, there's no telling what I might do next: pick flowers for a nice bouquet, gaze wistfully out the window— sick and twisted behavior.

First Dates

After you've formed an unshakable crush, you can ask them on a date. Some good first dates include counting the rings on an old oak tree, getting the same haircut, and mating.

An outfit can make or break your date.
Try to select something both smart and
comfortable. I could wear my suit and
tie, but if the waistcoat bunches around
my underarms, I'm going to misbehave
the whole time. Pick a look that says
"I've been on a sailboat before," but in a
totally casual way.

On a date, it is customary to tell a few jokes. If my date does not laugh, I tell them it's a poem. A poem is a joke that isn't funny.

Being Single

Being unwed is underrated. There are many perks. For instance, you never have to double your oatmeal recipe. You get to pick all the area rugs in your cottage. You have plenty of time to put little ships in glass bottles. Sure, it's nice to go through life with another creature by your side, but just think of all the looking at moss-covered rocks you could get done on your own.

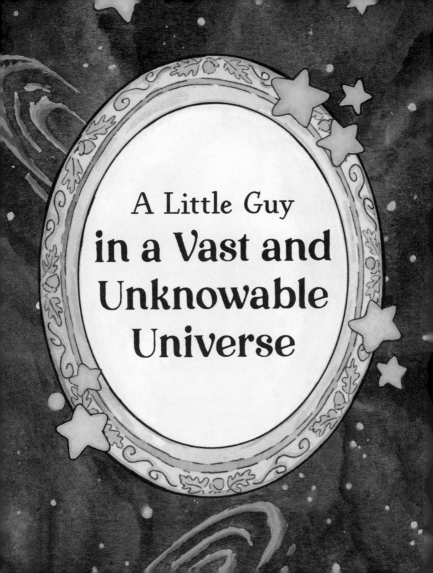

A Little Guy in a Vast and Unknowable Universe

A little guy is small. The universe is big. Too big, in my opinion, but nobody put me in charge of picking the sizes of things.

The Big Questions

Though this might come as a surprise, I do not have all the answers. There are birdbaths I haven't splashed in and riddles no one has explained to me. There are only two things I know for certain: what I'm having for dinner (soup) and what I'm having for lunch the next day (leftover soup).

Stargazing

When I feel myself getting too metaphorically big for my metaphorical britches, I like to look up at the stars to remind myself I am but a tadpole in the stream of life.

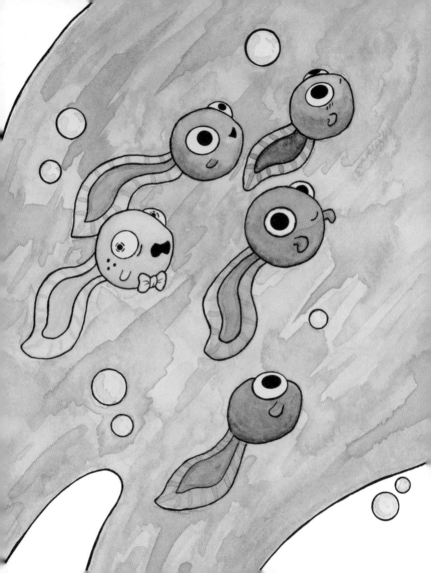

I recommend bringing a thick quilt and a friend who's good at pointing and going "Look!"

This is a nighttime activity. During the day, stars are busy being diamonds.

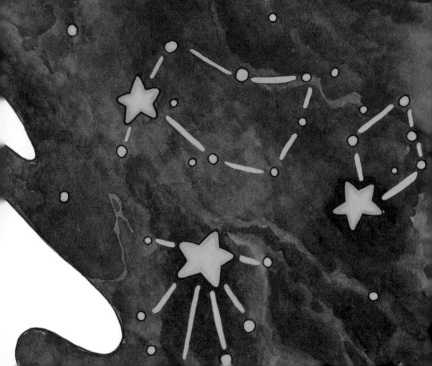

Anxiety

Sometimes things are bad. Worse, however, is when things might be bad soon.

If you are unfamiliar with anxiety, there are several ways you can trigger this feeling . . .

Drink a cappuccino on an empty
stomach and visit a ceramics studio with
no public restroom.

Drop your corncob pipe in a storm drain.

Tell your mother something about yourself.

My only advice for limiting anxiety is to spend fifty to ninety percent of your life supine near a large body of water.

Finding a Therapist

If you've already tried speaking directly into a wishing well to no avail, I suggest talking to a wise old owl or a professional therapist (interchangeable). Try not to pay out of pocket for therapy. Most small frog pockets are already full to the brim with stamps and smooth rocks anyway.

Screaming

Sometimes there is nothing more to do but scream. Locate the moon and howl to your heart's content. If it's daytime, check to see if the moon is out. If she is unavailable, you may scream into a deep well.

Fear of Death

When I was first informed that I will one day die, I was not pleased. Having sat with this fact for several years, I am still perturbed.

There's really no getting around it:
Everything alive will stop being alive.
Logs were trees, dead flowers were alive
flowers, and bones were guys we knew.
For this, I have no remedy except to say I
am glad to have witnessed the trees and
flowers and guys. It's all very nice while
it lasts.

As for what happens after we die, that's not my business. I'm sure I'll find out when I get dead, but right now I'm preoccupied with several things. Today, there are pants that need patching and sailboats that need looking at.